The Many Faces of

## Michael JACKSON

Created by Pop Culture,
published by Ozone Books a division of Bobcat Books, distributed by
Book Sales Ltd.  Newmarket Rd, Bury St Edmunds, Suffolk IP33 3YB.
Copyright © 1997 Pop Culture
Order No. 0Z100023
ISBN: 0-7119-6783-0

The author and publisher have made every effort to contact all
copyright holders. Any, who for whatever reason have not been
contacted are invited to write to the publishers so that so that a full
acknowledgement may be made in subsequent editions of this work

Picture credits: Redferns, All Action, Rex features, Angela Lubrano,
Steve Double.

Design by:

*The Many Faces of*

# Michael JACKSON

by Lee Pinkerton

# *Introduction*

Michael Jackson is the most commercially successful recording artist of all time. He has sold more than 210 million records and has won over 60 awards. But as we all know he is much more than just a singer. He is a dancer, choreographer, songwriter, producer, visionary, filmmaker and humanitarian. His music and videos have touched so many people that he can now no longer even be regarded as a mere recording artist - he is a pop culture phenomenon.

He has been recording since the age of 5, breaking records since the age of 11, and been a star without equal since he turned 21. His album 'Thriller' has sold more than any other album in recording history. In 1983 he won more Grammy's than any other artist in any other year. In 1991 he signed the biggest recording deal in music business history and has earned more money than any other pop star in the nineties. As well as his sounds being record breaking he is also a visual wonder. He has been so influential on the making of pop videos that music television station MTV renamed their Video Vanguard Award the Michael Jackson Video Vanguard and he has played more dates at Wembley stadium than any other artist. And yet despite living his life in the public eye people still have an insatiable desire to find out more about him. His autobiography 'Moonwalk' was the No.1 book in America and Britain and has sold in excess of 450,000 copies in fourteen countries around the world.

His appeal goes across racial, religious, geographical, language, generation, gender, and musical boundaries. And he himself has broken down a few barriers. He was the first black artist to receive extensive airplay on MTV. People who were originally fans of his when they were children now have kids of their own who are fans. It is impossible to explain the phenomenal appeal of this man, probably not even Michael himself knows. But what we can give you is an insight into the life of the man and his music...

In August 1958 Michael Joseph Jackson was born to father Joe and mother Katherine, the seventh child in an already large family. He joined two sisters (Maureen and La Toya) and four brothers (Jackie, Tito, Jermaine and Marlon). Janet and Randy were still to come. Michael's father Joe worked as a crane operator in the steel mills in Gary, Indiana where the family lived. In the 1950's he had aspirations of going into show business, and even had his own group called The Falcons but with the responsibility of eleven mouths to feed Joe had to put his musical aspirations on hold.

As the legend has it, it was when Michael's older brother Tito was caught with his father's guitar that Joe discovered the brothers had some real musical talent. A family group was formed in the household and although he was aged only 6 his talent was so self-evident that it was decided that little Michael would be the lead singer. This meant that Joe had to split the money between feeding the family and buying the group instruments.

## The Jackson Five Are Born

A woman in the neighbourhood soon came up with the name The Jackson Five, and they began practising every day after school. Father Joe was a hard taskmaster and this meant they could not go out and play with the other children and consequently were teased. But the Jackson brothers remained happy because they were doing something that they loved. Their father then entered them onto the local talent show circuit, and when Michael was 8 they won a major contest with their rendition of The Temptations 'My Girl'. By now Joe had gone part-time at the mill and was managing the band full time. He booked them in for their first professional gigs at a local nightclub; Mr Lucky's where they earned $8 a night for five sets, six or sometimes seven nights a week. Then, in the winter of 1967

**5**

they cut their first record, a simple R&B number called 'Big Boy', which was released in 1968 on the Steeltown label. It was a small hit in the local Gary charts and in a few neighbouring towns. When they won the Royal Theatre Amateur Night for three weeks in a row they also won the right to do a proper paid show there. The group got their first taste of the big time when they opened up for the headlining Gladys Knight and The Pips.

But it was not until 1968 that they got their chance to play at the legendary Amateur Night at the Apollo in New York. Of course they won and during the following months they continued touring the country in their small Volkswagen minivan waiting to get that big break. It came when they got a chance to audition for Berry Gordy the head of Motown records, the most successful Black music label ever.

After the audition came the waiting. Jackie remembers not being able to use the phone for two months while they were waiting for the label to call. However, call they did and the Jackson Five were signed to Motown Records.

## Motown's New Signings

Diana Ross had not discovered The Jackson Five as the publicity had stated but she took a profound interest in their development. She became a second mother to Michael, allowing him and some his brothers to live with her whilst their mother Katherine stayed in Indiana looking after La Toya, Randy and Janet. Only after the success of The Jackson Five's first single did Joe bring the whole family out to California to live.

The group's first album, 'Diana Ross presents The Jackson Five', was released in December 1969 and the band went on to be the fastest selling group in the history of Motown Records. Oddly, only one song was released from their debut album, 'I Want You back' which sold two million copies in six weeks, staying in the US Billboard charts for sixteen weeks and reaching No.1 at the end of January 1970. At the time Jackie was 18, Tito was 16, Jermaine was 15, Marlon was 12, and Michael was already a seasoned performer at the age of 11.

Over the next year three more Motown albums were released by The Jackson Five. No sooner than 'I Want You Back' began to descend, the title song of their second album 'ABC' was released. Again the song shot up to the top of the charts as did its follow up 'The Love You Save'. The group finished 1970 with four No.1 hit singles, four albums, and a following of devoted fans that stretched out around the world. Not bad for a first year. 1971 was even bigger. There were another three albums, three more No.1 singles, their own network television special, a concert tour, their own animated cartoon series, and a cover story in Life magazine. Spring 1971 brought two more chart hits and then in the summer of the same year they followed it up with a tour that took them to Britain for their first concert abroad.

# Michael Goes Solo

After the initial success of the Jackson Five, Berry Gordy began trying to persuade Michael to try a song on his own. His very first solo release was the single 'Got To Be There' which was released in October 1971 and peaked at No.4 in the charts. 'Got To Be There' was also the name of his first solo album released in February 1972 and made it to No. 3 in the Black charts and No.14 in the pop charts. Now Motown had a No.1 single from Michael they persevered, changing the style around with the three songs that followed. Michael's second solo enterprise 'Rockin' Robin' reached No. 2, but the next two failed to reach the Top Ten. The breakthrough came with an ode to a rat. 'Ben' was the theme song to a film about a boy who shared his difficult life with his best friend a pet rat. The song went to No.1 in the US and No.7 in the UK and easily eclipsed the success of the film.

## Back As A Group

In late 1972 and early 1973 The Jackson Five toured the world starting in England where they met the Queen, and visiting Africa, Japan, China and Australia. In 1974 they played in Las Vegas and in 1975 Michael released another solo album 'Forever Michael', that was to be his last original Motown album to be released. It also contained the single that would be become an UK hit years later, 'One Day In Your Life'. 'Moving Violation', also released in 1975 was the last Jackson Five album released on Motown. The label still wanted them to record songs written and produced by the Motown in house team but they wanted to start writing and performing their own songs. Motown would not even let them play their own instruments in the recording sessions. Joe Jackson, their father and manager wanted more money. A split was imminent.

## The Five Leave Motown

In March 1976 Joe Jackson held a press conference to announce that The Jackson Five would not be renewing their contract with Motown. Even though Motown demanded that they complete another album to fulfill their contract, Jackson refused to comply. Since Motown claimed it owned the name 'The Jackson Five' they

had to leave it with them. They also left behind their brother Jermaine, who had married Berry Gordy's daughter Hazel and stayed loyal to the family label. Whilst Michael, Jackie, Tito, Marlon, and Randy, signed with CBS records subsidiary Epic, Jermaine signed a solo deal with Motown.

A legal battle ensued between Motown and Epic that would take some five years to settle.

The brother's first solo album for Epic was entitled simply 'The Jacksons' and was released in November 1976. For it, they linked up with hit making, writing and production duo Gamble and Huff and also had the opportunity to write their own compositions. The second album entitled 'Goin' Places', released in 1977, was again produced by Gamble and Huff and contained two Jackson compositions. On the bad side, they were now having problems. The first two Epic albums had not been successful and the label was getting worried. In 1978 their third CBS album 'Destiny' was released, it was the first album for which they had complete creative control and with the exception of one track all the songs were written by the group. The album also contained their biggest hit for some time, one of Michael's compositions, 'Shake Your Body (Down To The Ground)'. The album was eventually certified Platinum - 1 million copies sold. Michael, having saved his brothers with his song writing abilities, once again began to focus his attention on a solo career.

# Off the Wall 1979

## A Man Named Quincy

In 1978 Michael appeared in 'The Wiz', a black film version of the Hollywood classic 'The Wizard of Oz'. It was whilst working on this movie that he met Quincy Jones - Michael had starred as the Scarecrow and Quincy had worked as the movie's musical director. Michael asked Quincy to recommend a producer that he could work with on his first solo album for Epic and Quincy volunteered himself. Michael's only requisite was that the music should not sound like the Jacksons' and before long Quincy had gotten together a selection of top class songs and a set of the very best studio musicians.

With the producer and the musicians sorted, what they needed now was the songs. Michael was very anxious to prove himself as a solo artist and also to do the kind of ballads that he did not feel he could do within the group.

The search for songs brought together Michael with another greatly talented songwriter; the two were to become firm friends. Paul McCartney gave Michael a song after inviting him to a party at his house. The 'Off The Wall' album was originally going to be called 'Girlfriend' after the song that McCartney had written for Michael. However, the team obviously felt that 'Off The Wall' reflected the approach of the album, having an altogether more modern feel than anything that The Jacksons had made as a group. It had the funky feel of the 1970's but also a modern electric feel that ushered in the 1980's.

Another very successful pairing was with Rod Temperton who wrote the title track, as well as 'Rock With You', and 'Burn This Disco Out'. Michael wrote three of the songs himself and Stevie Wonder also contributed a song entitled 'I Can't Help It'.

## State Of Independence

The album was a major step for Michael. He had done solo albums before with Motown but those were written and produced by the label's team with Michael's only contribution being the singing. 'Off The Wall' was his own project following his own vision. It was a visual statement as well as a musical one. Michael appeared on the cover wearing a tuxedo but with his own individual touch of white fluorescent socks. His nose was also discernably thinner; indicating the first of Michael's dalliances with cosmetic surgery.

In September 1979 the first single from the album was released. ' Don't Stop Till You Get Enough' went straight in at No.1 in the States and went to No.3 in the UK. It was a song that Michael was understandably proud of as it was the first he had written

entirely by himself and it also featured his own overdubbed vocals which in effect meant that he was also doing his own backing singing.

Also co-producing three of the tracks with Quincy gave Michael the musical freedom that he had been looking for. The second single release 'Rock With You'/ 'Working Day And Night' followed 'Don't Stop...' to the No.1 spot. Perhaps the most memorable track was released in May of 1980. 'She's Out Of My Life' was a song about the pain of lost love. When Michael performed it in the studio he got so involved in the emotion of the song that he broke down and cried at the very last line. So they recorded it again.

*"Every time we did it I'd look up at the end and Michael would be crying,"* recalls Quincy. *"I said we'll come back in two weeks and do it again and maybe it won't tear you up so much. Came back and he started to get teary. So we left it in."*

When the third and fourth singles off the album both hit the Top Ten 'Off The Wall' made musical history and Michael went onto win a Grammy Award for Best Male R&B Vocal Performance.

In Britain the McCartney track 'Girlfriend' also charted, this was the first time that five chart hits came from one album thus setting a new record. The album sold five million copies in the United States and eight million world-wide.

To add to the continuing Jackson mania, Michael and The Jacksons released their fourth CBS album entitled 'Triumph'. It was again written and produced by the band. To capitalise on the resurgence of interest in Michael and The Jacksons from 1979 - 1981 Motown released two albums by Michael and two by The Jackson Five.

Also in 1980 another member of the Jackson family, La Toya released her first solo album on the Polydor label containing two tracks that were written and produced by Michael.

1981 was a very significant year for Michael. It was the year in which he got his very first solo No.1 in Britain, (even though it was a song recorded years ago) when Motown re-issued 'One Day In Your Life'. Now Michael was a major star. After getting back together with his brothers to record 'Triumph' Michael went on a thirty-nine-city concert tour with them in 1981. When they played Madison Square Garden, in New York amongst the stars in attendance were artist Andy Warhol, comedian Dan Aykroyd, Jane Fonda, film director Steven Spielberg, singer Andy Gibb, and actors Katherine Hepburn, Victoria Principal, Tatum O' Neal, and Jamie Lee Curtis. A two album set 'The Jacksons Live' was released and recorded to capture the event. However, the best was yet to come.

# Thriller

During 1982 Michael Jackson was involved with three different recording projects. He produced and wrote the song 'Muscles' for Diana Ross, he sang on and narrated the storybook album, 'E.T. The Extra Terrestrial' and recorded his second solo album for Epic records. For his album he once again asked Quincy Jones to produce (why break up a winning team?) and the duo then set about looking for songs.

## The Search For Songs

He contacted Paul McCartney and this led to a visit to the ex-Beatle's Scottish farm where the two artists wrote several numbers. Two of them appeared on McCartney's 'Pipes Of Peace' album over a year later but one 'The Girl Is Mine' was picked out for Michael's album. Another 300 songs were considered. On the finished album Rod Temperton provided three songs, 'Baby be Mine', 'The Lady In My Life' and 'Thriller' which became the title track. Michael himself provided 'Startin' Something', 'Billie Jean' and 'Beat It'. Heavy metal guitarist Eddie Van Halen was drafted in to play on the latter, giving it an authentic rock feel and expanding Michael's fan base to include the rock crowd. The lead single off the album, the duet with McCartney was already well up in the charts when the album was released in December 1982 in time for the Christmas rush.

## Video Star

But it was not just good timing or good songs that pushed the 'Thriller' album to the No.1 spot. By the 1980's American music station MTV had become a major force and the pop video an integral part of the marketing of a record. Michael was one of the first artists to acknowledge this. Unfortunately, at that time MTV was still very much a rock station and had an unofficial ban on Black music - the only Black artist to have made it onto MTV at the time was Tina Turner on a light rotation basis. It required major force exerted by Michael's record company to get the video for 'Billie Jean' played and that was only after the single had already become a hit.

In the 'Billie Jean' video the world could now see Michael's new image for the 1980's. He had gone from the soft perm of 'Off The Wall' to a new wet-look hairstyle, plucked eyebrows, eyeliner, slick dance

moves and even slicker clothes. Michael dressed in Black leather trousers, black leather jacket, pink shirt and red bow tie, lighting up the street wherever he walked. The story for the video showed Michael being trailed by a seedy private eye - no doubt hired to uncover dirt on Michael - but Michael Jackson is always one step ahead.

It was Michael's electrifying live performance of 'Billie Jean' at 1983's Motown 25th Anniversary special that sent sales of the 'Thriller' album rising again just as they were starting to slump. The video for 'Beat It' was similarly stunning, filmed on the streets of Los Angeles and featuring a choreographed ensemble dance piece that has since become a staple of music videos. The theme of gang warfare in the video has prompted it to be compared to a mini-version of 'West Side Story' but it was certainly an epic milestone in music videos. Some actual Los Angeles street gang members were used along side the professional dancers to give it an authentic feel and it cost $100,000 to make.

During the summer of 1983 three more singles were released and all went Top Ten in the states.

Then came the video to top them all. 'Thriller' was directed by John Landis. Michael had seen his film 'American Werewolf in London' and felt that Landis was the perfect person to realise the ideas he had for the 'Thriller' video. It employed some of the same ground breaking special effects that were used in the Landis movie and was a pastiche of horror movie themes such as werewolves and zombies, as well as including Michael's ensemble dance pieces.

The video was revolutionary, totally reworking the song in order to tell a story, firstly of Michael as the lead character of a 1950's werewolf B movie, then to the present day with Michael walking his date home from seeing the Werewolf movie. During the course of which he encounters a crew of zombies in a dark alley and Jackson himself becomes one. It ran for 15 minutes and a short film of the making of the video was released which became a best seller in its own right, being the first music video to go platinum. All this was of course good for the sales of the album that continued to rise. *"I wanted 'Thriller' and 'Beat It' to be a stimulant for people to make better videos or short films,"* said Michael at the time.

## A Good Year

Michael ended the year by holding No.1 spots in both the Album and Singles charts with 'Say, Say, Say' and 'Thriller'.

In America Michael was also the first act to have three No.1 hits during one calendar year. 'Thriller' spent all fifty-two weeks of 1983 in the Top Ten of the Albums chart in the US, thirty-seven weeks of which were spent at No.1. It also became the first album in the history of recorded music to begin and end the year at No. 1.

Meanwhile Michael and The Jacksons had signed a lucrative advertising contract with Pepsi and in January 1984 started filming the television adverts. It was during this filming that one of the lighting effects sent a spark into his hair causing it to catch alight. Subsequently he was rushed to hospital with second-degree burns. However, he was well enough to attend the prestigious Grammy Awards a month later in February having been nominated for twelve categories. He attended the ceremony with Brooke Shields and went onto win a record breaking eight out of the twelve awards he was nominated for, including: Album Of The Year and Single Of The Year for 'Beat It'. The album went onto break many other records, most notably being the top selling album of all time, shifting forty-two million units.

# Bad

Despite the enormous success of 'Thriller' Michael still remained loyal to his family and agreed to go on tour with the his brothers again. However there were problems from the start. From the age of 21 Michael had taken over his own business affairs whilst his brothers were still managed by their father. A stream of promoters were hired and then fired rendering the event an organisational nightmare. Michael cheered himself up in the spring of 1984 by having another nose alteration, adding a little flare and a slight turn up.

Eventually Michael and his brothers went into the studio to record their new album 'Victory' and in May 1984 rehearsals for the tour started. Elaborate ticket purchasing guidelines were announced and over a million were sold in just two months, however in July, after receiving a letter from a distraught fan who accused The Jacksons and the promoters of being selfish and just out for the money, Michael held a press conference. He announced changes to the tour's organisation and also that the whole of his share of the profits would be donated to his three favourite charities - a fund for college education to help underprivileged black students, a holiday camp for sick children, and for cancer and leukaemia research.

In September in the middle of the tour Michael called another press conference, this time to dispel rumours about his personal life. Although not present in person Michael's two page statement was read out by his manager Frank Dileo. It stated that from here on, he was prepared to sue all those who continued to perpetuate lies about him. The 'Victory Tour' ran for fifty-five dates across America, from July to December, but Michael was said to be relieved when it came to an end in Los Angeles. *"It's been a long 20 years,"* he said on stage that night. *"This is our final farewell tour as a family."*

## We Are The World

Once home he began working on his next solo project but a number of other projects came about to distract him. The first was USA for Africa in January 1985, a project inspired by the UK's Band Aid record. The lyrics were written in collaboration with Lionel Richie. Other stars that performed on the record included Bob Dylan, Bruce Springsteen, Cyndi Lauper, and Diana Ross. Michael's old friend Quincy Jones was musical arranger. The next project was to create a ride for Disneyland. The 3D movie spectacular 'Captain EO' cost $30 million dollars to make and was directed by Francis Ford Coppola, of 'Godfather' fame and also involved 'Star Wars' producer George Lucas. For much of the next two years he was in the studio working on his next album.

# Bad

Once again Quincy Jones was chosen as producer. Michael's confidence as a songwriter had grown since the success of 'Thriller' so there was not a repeat of the massive search for songs as there had been on previous albums. On 'Bad' Michael wrote eight of the ten songs himself. One of the others, 'Man In The Mirror' came from session singer and songwriter Siedah Garrett. The appeal of that song won her the chance to duet with Michael on the track 'I Just Can't Stop Loving You' - an opportunity that strangely had already been turned down by Barbra Streisand and Whitney Houston.

For the title track 'Bad', top film director and friend of Quincy, Martin Scorcese was chosen to shoot the video. Another mini movie, it cost over $2 million dollars to make and told the story of Daryl, a Black youth from the ghetto who returns home from his private prep school to find that he no longer fits in. Loosely based on a true story and reminiscent of 'Beat It's' hard inner city edge, the anti-violence message was again reflected in gangland dance scenes. Though visually it was reminiscent of previous songs Michael had a completely new image. Michael wore a black leather motorcycle outfit, complete with multiple studded belts and buckles. A publicity shot of Michael taken during the filming of the video was eventually used for the cover of the album. The video was given its first public airing in a 30 minute TV documentary -' Michael Jackson - The Magic Returns', aired in August. However, the 'Smooth Criminal' video, which cost $8 million, dwarfed the budget for the 'Bad' video. It seemed that movies inspired Michael's interest the most at this time and in March he went to work on another film project called 'Moonwalker'.

However, he did eventually get back to the album project and it was eventually finished in June of 1987 and released at the end of the year. In August the duet with Siedah Garrett, Michael's first single release for three years, went straight to No.1 in both the UK and US charts. When the album was released in the UK in September reports abounded of the opening day siege on record shops to purchase it. Tower Records in London sold 200 copies in the first hour. It went straight to No.1 and stayed there for five weeks, its sales exceeding the whole of the rest of the Top Forty. Throughout its first week one in every four albums sold was 'Bad'. 'Thriller' and 'Off the Wall' also re-entered the album charts in Britain.

In October the second single 'Bad' followed the album to No.1. It yielded another three No.1s, sold 11 million copies around the world and reached No.1 in twenty-three countries. Michael Jackson became the first artist to have four No.1 singles and the first to have four subsequent Top Ten hits from three consecutive albums.

## Bad Tour

In September 1987 he kicked off his first ever solo tour - 'The World Bad Tour' - in Japan with fourteen sell out concerts. The tour took in one hundred and twenty-three dates in fifteen countries on four continents over the next sixteen months. When tickets for Michael's 'Bad Tour' went on sale in Britain in November 1987, it was reported that the 144,000 tickets for Wembley Stadium sold out within three hours. Over 6,000 people queued outside Wembley's box office, many camping over night despite freezing temperatures.

In September 1988 Michael was presented with an award for setting a new record for playing more dates at Wembley Stadium than any other artist. Five hundred and four thousand people attended his seven sell out concerts - an achievement, which got him another place in the Guinness Book Of Records. After playing in England the 'Bad Tour' went back to America. He played the one hundred and twenty-third and final show - this was announced as the farewell concert - in January 1989 at the Los Angeles Sports Arena. 'The Bad World Tour' attendance figures totalled 4.4 million making Michael's sixteen-month tour the largest in history. It was also the highest grossing concert tour, raking in over $125 million.

# Dangerous

## Moonwalk

Despite the great demands of the 'Bad Tour' Michael found time to sit down and talk to a writer who turned their conversations into Michael Jackson's biography 'Moonwalk'. The book was edited by Jacqueline Onassis and topped the best seller list in Britain and the US in the summer of 1988. Michael dedicated the book to one of his all time idols, Fred Astaire. The film 'Moonwalker', an extravagant mix of music, dance and special effects was released on home video in time for Christmas 1988. A single from the film 'Leave Me Alone', about his treatment by the press, made No.2 in the UK charts in February 1989.

## Problems At Home

Meanwhile things were not so great at home. Whilst his 'Bad Tour' had been in Liverpool he phoned home to apologise for his portrayal of his father Joseph in the book. Joe had gone on to TV in April of 1988 denying the beatings that Michael spoke of in the book, describing them as little beatings. But in an interview brother Marlon defended Michael saying that they were hit - and often. Michael moved out of the family home in Hayvenhurst into the 2,700 acre ranch in the Santa Ynez Valley in California which he renamed the Neverland Valley Ranch.

Sister La Toya who was embarking on a solo career took inspiration from Michael and was writing an autobiography in which she accused their father of abusing the Jacksons as children. But the rest of the family immediately closed ranks to denounce it. The family strife continued as the Jacksons made an album without Michael, '2300 Jackson Street' which flopped. This album completed the group's contract with Epic records - a contract, which was not renewed. But worst of all Jermaine released a song 'Word To The Bad' which attacked Michael for his cosmetic surgery and resulted in him distancing himself from the family. On the BBC programme Rapido Jermaine explained why he wrote the song 'Word To The Bad'. *"I tried to put some phone calls to him and I didn't get a reply...it's a number of things but it's nothing that we couldn't have worked out had we spoken. But I wasn't granted an opportunity...the overall message is an older brother telling a younger brother to get back to reality."*

But it was not only the family that Michael was distancing himself from. In February 1989 he sacked his hard working manager for the last four years Frank Dileo as well as his lawyer John Branca. In June 1990 the stress and anxiety all proved too much and he collapsed whilst dancing in his home studio. He was ordered to rest before resuming work on the new album.

## New Album - New Approach.

During the 'Bad Tour' Michael had been writing songs and recording them in demo form. These songs were originally scheduled to appear on a double album called 'Decade' containing several new numbers alongside a handful of classic hits from the 1980's. Partly because of his personal upheaval and partly because he believed that there was enough material for a complete new album the idea for 'Decade' was scrapped, though it was one that sister Janet later took up for her 'Design Of A Decade' album released in 1995.

The 'Dangerous' album can be viewed in two distinct halves, perhaps acknowledging his two audiences. The first half attempted to get back to his roots in Black music. He dropped Quincy Jones in favour of hot new producer Teddy Riley. Riley was responsible for the new musical genre New Jack Swing (or Swingbeat as it was called in this country) a sound he had pioneered with R&B artists such as Keith Sweat, Bobby Brown and Guy. In keeping with this new approach the album for the first time also featured rappers, Heavy D appearing on the track 'Jam'. The video also featured basketball superstar Michael Jordan.

## The Videos

The back-to-Black policy was also reflected in the video for 'Remember The Time' which featured top Black comedian Eddie Murphy, top Black model Iman, top Black basketball player Magic Johnson, and was directed by Black director John Singleton.

The video for 'Keep It In The Closet' featured Black British supermodel Naomi Campbell. The second half of the 'Dangerous' album was back to the pop rock that had worked on 'Beat It', and 'Bad' with tracks like 'Black Or White' and 'Give In To Me', which had special guitar appearances by Guns & Roses guitarist Slash. Then there was 'Heal The World', 'Keep The Faith' and 'Gone Too Soon' - anthems for the planet and the world's children that have since become a Michael trademark. 'Will You Be There' was another spiritual number with orchestral and choral arrangements. When he sang it on MTV's 10th birthday special surrounded by a choir of children it left many of the audience close to tears.

The video for 'Black Or White' the album's first single, was directed by John Landis who had done 'Thriller', and 500 million viewers were said to have seen it in its first week of release. The video featured Macaulay Culkin, Michael's niece Brandi, Bart Simpson, George Wendt (who played Norm in Cheers) and rapper Heavy D. It finished with a four minute

DANGEROUS

dance sequence with no music, which showed Michael smashing up a car. The BBC refused to show it on television describing it as gratuitous violence not suitable for family viewing and many television stations missed out the last part. Then Sony records arranged an elaborate world-wide synchronised play for the single. Copies of the single given to radio stations in major cities were played at exactly the same time. It went straight in at No.1, holding its position for two weeks. It was the first single to enter the charts at the top spot since 1969, when Elvis, for the second and last time, accomplished it with 'It's Now Or Never'. The album went on sale in November 1991 and turned triple platinum after only three weeks.

## Cover Art

Instead of the simple photographs that had adorned previous covers 'Dangerous' featured a complex painting by artist Mark Ryden, a composite of images many of which had been included at Michael's request. By the end of February 1992 it had sold more than ten million copies world-wide. In the same month Michael Jackson made an announcement that came as something of a surprise considering the announcement he had made three years before. He wanted to go back on stage and do a world tour. It was to be the greatest show on earth with theatrical performances that recreated his epic videos. All the profits would go to his new charitable foundation Heal The World. In June 1992 he started his 'Dangerous World Tour' in Munich, Germany and taking in Britain, France, Romania, before medical problems with his vocal cords cut his tour short. He resumed it in December performing in Japan.

## From Bad To Better

Due to Michael's recent album release, his world tour, his health scare, and the antics of the rest of his family, Michael and the Jacksons had never been far from the news. However, since Michael had been refusing to give interviews for the last few years the press was left to write whatever they wanted. In 1993, probably in an attempt to counteract the negative publicity, Michael Jackson took up a new and more open position with the media.

In January he attended two award shows, receiving awards from the NAACP and the American Music Awards and joined other celebrities in the inaugural celebrations of newly elected President Bill Clinton. He also performed a medley of his hits 'Jam', 'Billie Jean', 'Black Or White' and 'Heal The World' at the Super Bowl Half time Show in the Rose Bowl Stadium in California.

In February Michael Jackson Talks... to Oprah was telecast live from his home in Neverland Valley attracting around 100 million viewers around the world. Michael refused to answer questions about allegations made by La Toya in her book, saying he hadn't read it, and also declined to disclose as to whether he was a virgin or not. But he did reveal that he did not really know his father, and that he suffered from the skin disease, Vitiligo which destroys the pigmentation in his skin.

With his new spirit of glasnost sales of 'Dangerous' increased dramatically. After his performance at the Superbowl, 'Dangerous' moved up the US Albums chart an amazing one hundred and six places from No.131 to No.41. After the Oprah interview the album rose another thirty-one places to No.10 more than a year after its release. In Britain 'Dangerous' rose to No.6 in the Top Seventy-five Albums chart.

In February he was at another awards ceremony, this time the Grammy Awards, where he was nominated in two categories, neither of which he won. He was however presented with a Grammy Legend Award by his sister Janet. He said at the time, *"In the past month I have gone from where is he? To where is he again. But I must confess it feels good to be thought of as a person, not as a personality. Because I don't read all the things written about me I wasn't aware that the world thought I was so weird and so bizarre, but when you grow up as I did, in front of one hundred million people since the age of 5, you're automatically different. The last few weeks I have been cleansing myself and it's been a rebirth for myself. It's like a cleansing spirit."*

Following the presentation Michael and his date Brooke Shields attended the Polygram party at A&M Studios and later showed up at the Sony Music Party in Centaury City.

# History

Things seemed to be going well for Michael in 1993. 'The Dangerous Tour' was generally acclaimed to be one of the most spectacular ever and sales of the album, although not as great as 'Bad' and certainly not in the league of 'Thriller', were still rising. In addition to that he won a number of awards and his new open attitude to the media seemed to be winning him better coverage. But then in the summer of 1993 it all went horribly wrong. Michael was rocked by the worst scandal of his life.

## Criminal Investigations

In August 17th the Los Angeles Police Department officially opened a criminal investigation on Michael based on allegations of child abuse made by a 13 year old boy, Jordy Chandler. Four days later the LAPD served search warrants on Jackson's Neverland Valley Ranch in Santa Barbara, California, and on his condominium in Century City, California. Boxes of photographs and video tapes are reported to have been removed from each home.

At this time Michael was on the Asian leg of the 'Dangerous Tour' kicking off in Bangkok, moving to Singapore, Moscow and Istanbul. As reports surfaced that Michael was under criminal investigation, Michael's own investigator Anthony Pellicano argued that the accusations were the result of a failed attempt to extort money from Michael.

Two young friends came to Michael's defence telling police and the media that he never behaved inappropriately with them. However, their admissions to having shared a bed with Michael - in a friendly slumber party spirit - only caused more damage.

## Michael Jackson Under Stress

Back in Asia Michael's health was suffering. His first concert in Bangkok was postponed due to dehydration, as was his second one in Singapore when he collapsed backstage. After having a brain scan and taking a short break he resumed the tour going to Brazil and Mexico. But by November Michael cancelled the rest of the tour explaining that due to the stress he was under he had become addicted to painkillers and needed to seek treatment. His whereabouts in the world at this point were

a mystery and rumours started to circulate that he was in hiding or that he was undergoing cosmetic surgery to alter his appearance. Michael's 'Greatest Hits' album, containing three new songs which had been planned for release in 1993 had to be postponed as Michael had not finished recording the new tracks and a new release date was tentatively set for June 1994.

## Public Reactions - Child Abuse Allegations

His label, Sony Music, issued a statement of unconditional support, but his biggest sponsors Pepsi were reluctant to do the same. Police then obtained a warrant to strip search Michael in an effort to verify the description of his genitalia given by Michael's accusers. The UK's quality newspapers took a dubious stance, but the tabloid newspapers screamed outrage, convicting Michael before any trial. The Jackson family stood by him, Jermaine threatening to sue one newspaper for $200 million for publishing a story saying that he questioned Michael's innocence. Sister La Toya, however, did not join in this united front, shocking the world by saying she could no longer be a silent conspirator to her brother's crimes. In December Michael Jackson finally returned to the States and on December 22nd went on television to make a public statement.

## Public Statement

In the statement Michael declared his innocence and revealed the humiliating examination that he was subjected to by the County Sheriffs Office. They served a search warrant on him which allowed them to examine and photograph his genitalia, his buttocks and any other part of his body they

wished. They were looking for signs of blotches or other evidence of the skin disorder Vitiligo which he had spoken of previously.

Michael said in his televised statement: *"It was the most humiliating ordeal of my life - one that no person should ever have to suffer. It was a nightmare, a horrifying nightmare. But if this is what I have to endure to prove my innocence, my complete innocence, then so be it. I shall not in this statement respond to all the false allegations being made against me, since my lawyers have advised me that this is not the proper forum in which to do that. I will say that I am particularly upset by the handling of this matter by the incredible and terrible mass media. At every opportunity the media has dissected and manipulated these allegations to reach their own conclusions. I ask all of you to wait to hear the truth before you label or condemn me. Don't treat me like a criminal because I am innocent."*

## Out Of Court

However, Michael never got a chance to prove his innocence in court. In January the LAPD prosecutors announced that they did not have enough evidence to charge Evan Chandler - the boy's father with extortion and two days later, after six months of hard negotiations the lawyers representing both sides in the molestation case reached an agreement. An out of court settlement, which both sides had been working towards, was agreed for an undisclosed sum. The next day Reuters News Service

reported that the photos taken of Michael's genitalia did not match the accuser's description. Many felt at the time that if Michael truly was innocent then he should relish the opportunity to clear his name in court. However, it was recognised that Michael being such a private person could not bear to have his personal life exposed to the world in a media circus of a trial. The next year in an interview with his new wife Lisa Marie Presley he revealed the reasoning behind his actions. *"I asked my lawyer if he could guarantee me that justice would prevail. He said that he could not guarantee what a judge or jury would do. So I said that I have got to do something to get out of this nightmare... all these people were coming forward to get paid on these tabloid TV shows. And its lies, lies, lies. So I got together with my advisors and they advised me in an unanimous decision to resolve the case. It could go on for 7 years."*

## *His Side of The Story*

Still, after the media circus with everyone from Michael's family, ex-employees, to young friends all having their say, people still wanted to hear Michael's side of the story. He told them in the best way he knew how - through his music. But it was feared by many that the recent scandal that Michael had suffered would adversely effect his record sales. So his label, which had promised to stand by him, pulled out all the stops in a promotional campaign to eclipse all others.

'HIStory: Past Present And Future' was released around the world in June 1995. It was a double album divided into two segments: 'HIStory Begins' and 'HIStory Continues'. The former was a collection of fifteen of Michael's all time greatest hits including 'Beat It', 'Billie Jean', 'Thriller', 'Bad', and 'Black Or White'. 'HIStory Continues' had fifteen new recordings giving a total of 150 minutes of music. Many of the new songs like 'Scream', 'Money', 'Stranger In Moscow', 'Smile' and 'Tabloid Junkie', could be seen as his comments on the events in his life over the last two years.

*"This is an intensely personal record,"* said David Glew, Chairman of the Epic Group, announcing the release. *"His lyrics can be taken as a response to the situations that have overtaken his life in the last couple of years. It's a message from Michael to the public delivered in the only way that it can be delivered: through Michael's music."*

It certainly was his most autobiographical album to date and tracks like 'Earth Song' and 'They Don't Care About Us', showed a new angry socially aware side to Michael.

## The Promotion

All formats of the album included a fifty-two-page four-colour booklet. Epic records designed an eighteen month global strategy to promote the album. Statues of Michael constructed by his record company were unveiled in several European cities to herald its release. The 300 foot tall Monument To Victory statue in Volgograd, Russia, inspired this same statue that featured on the album's cover. To develop an image for the cover of superior quality and realism, Sony Music art directors turned to special effects specialist company Kleiser-Walczak Construction known for their work on the motion pictures 'Stargate' and 'Honey I Blew Up The Kids'.

## The Music

On this album Michael Jackson continued some trends and had a number of firsts. He continued his trend from 'Dangerous' by using guest rappers - this time hot newcomer Notorious B.I.G., rapping basketball player Shaquille O Neal, and in a show of family unity, for the first time, he performed a duet with his sister Janet. It was also the first time that he worked with young gun producer Dallas Austin and the production/songwriting duo, who had had such success with Janet, Jimmy Jam and Terry Lewis. He also performed a song written and produced by new R&B sensation R. Kelly. The album continued the convention from 'Dangerous' of making the album half R&B, half pop rock.

The first single to be released from the album was 'Scream' and entered the UK charts at No.3, and in America it debuted at No.5 making it the highest debut in the 37 year history of the Hot 100. That record was soon broken by the next single, the R. Kelly composition 'You Are Not Alone' which went straight in at No.1 in the US and entered the UK charts at No.3, but reached the top spot a week later. The video for the single featured Michael with his new wife Lisa Marie Presley. The album sold 7.5 million copies world-wide in only five weeks and eventually went onto sell fourteen million copies world-wide. In 1996 Michael started his 'HIStory' world tour in Eastern Europe.

# Blood on the Dancefloor 1997

On May 14th 1997 Epic records released Michael Jackson's sixth album for the label 'Blood On The Dancefloor' - 'HIStory In The Mix'. The album included five new songs and eight remixes of songs taken from Michael's multi-platinum album 'HIStory - Past, Present and Future'.

On this album more than ever before Michael acknowledged the dancefloor and the club crowd, who have become so important in the 1990's. Among the remixers included were: Jimmy Jam and Terry Lewis, Terry Farley and Pete Heller, Wyclef Jean and Pras of the Refugee Camp, Todd Terry, David Morales, Hani, Frankie Knuckles, and Tony Moran. They helped give new leases of life to the tracks 'Stranger In Moscow', 'Scream', 'Money', 'Bad', 'Earthsong' and 'You Are Not Alone'. Amongst the five new tracks Michael rejoined with producers he had worked with previously like Teddy Riley (who he had worked with on 'Dangerous') and Jimmy Jam and Terry Lewis (who he worked with on 'HIStory').

Michael and Teddy worked together on the track 'Ghost', which had been previously heard as the soundtrack for Michael's short film of the same name, which was released theatrically in the States in October 1996. It got its UK premier on 15th May 1997 at the Odeon Leicester Square at an event that was attended by media personalities, industry people and competition winners from his fan club. Michael meanwhile was unveiling the film at the Cannes Film Festival as part of the European launch of the album.

'Ghost' is a horror film showing Michael as the sole owner and resident of a haunted mansion, who one night receives a visit from a group of concerned locals and their children, who wish him to vacate their district for no other reason than he is strange - a freak. An angry white bigot, who is played by Michael himself in heavy make-up, leads the group. Scenes in the film of Michael dancing backed up by a band of ghouls are very reminiscent of his classic 'Thriller' video. Just as 'Thriller' took advantage of the best special effects available in the early 1980's, this video utilises the most advanced effects available today with Michael and his ghoulish friends getting up to all manner of supernatural tricks.

As well as appearing as a stout middle aged white man, Michael appears as a gigantic ghoul, and after tearing off his skin a dancing skeleton! In true Michael tradition 'Blood On The Dancefloor' went straight to No.1 in the Album charts in its first week

of release. Simultaneously released was a 'HIStory On Film Volume II' a compilation of Michael's greatest short films and award winning television performances.

# Michael the Business Man

Steven Spielberg said of Michael, *"He is one of the last living innocents who is in complete control of his life. I've never seen anybody like Michael. He's an emotional child star. He's in full control. Sometimes he appears to be wavering on the fringes of the twilight, but there is great conscious forethought behind everything he does. He's very smart about his career and the choices he makes. I think he is definitely a man of two personalities."*

People imagine Michael Jackson as someone out of touch with reality, with his head in the clouds. But when it comes to business Michael has got his feet firmly on the ground. Michael began to manage his own business interests at the age of 21 when his management contract with his father expired. Now as well as signing one of the most lucrative recording contracts ever, he is the owner of numerous, publishing catalogues, a record label, and a film company.

## Song Publishing

In August 1985, after ten months of negotiation he bought the massive music publishing back-catalogue of ATV (which includes most of The Beatles', Lennon and McCartney compositions) for more than $47 million. It sounds like a lot just for rights to some old songs but it means that whenever a Beatles' song is played on the radio, Michael gets some royalties. Whenever a cover version of a Beatles' song is made, or even sampled, permission has to be obtained from Michael and once again he gets a percentage of the royalties. The catalogue comprised of over four thousand compositions including two hundred and fifty one songs by The Beatles as well as hits by Little Richard, The Pointer Sisters, and The Pretenders. Michael was so pleased with his business success that he rewarded his attorney John Branca and manager Frank Dileo with a Rolls Royce each.

Here Michael put business before friendship, as he had to outbid his long-time friend Paul McCartney who also wished to obtain the rights. McCartney was said to be furious when he found out it was Michael who had outbid him for the rights, as he did not own the rights for many of his own songs.

However, McCartney has joined forces with the surviving group members a number of times to protect The Beatles' work. He successfully obtained a court order barring sales of three bootleg Beatles movies, and denied the Beastie Boys permission to use the Beatles song 'I'm Down' with new lyrics because they were too salacious. He did however allow the song 'Let It Be' to be re-recorded in aid of the Zeebrugge Tragedy Fund.

## Sponsorship

In March 1986 Michael received another placing in the Guinness Book of Records for the largest endorsement agreement in history between an individual and a major corporation, a reported $15 million dollars from Pepsi Cola, which he insisted on being paid up front in cash. But Pepsi could argue that it was money well spent. When the Michael Jackson advertisement premiered at the televised showing of the Grammy's in March 1988 they were so popular that they were requested by the Soviet officials to be aired on Soviet television. They were the first American advertisements to be aired in the Soviet Union and there were an estimated 150 million Soviet viewers.

In 1989 Michael Jackson signed a new endorsement deal with LA Gear. The two year deal required Michael to design and market a line of sports shoes and sportswear as well as appear in commercials. Under the special marketing campaign Unstoppable a wide range of activities were promised to promote the collection. But by the end of 1992 things had gone sour between Michael and the company. They sued him for $10 million. They had hoped to market the line of shoes to coincide with the release of a new Michael Jackson album, which was delayed. Michael in turn sued LA Gear for $44 million charging them with fraud and breach of contract.

## Earnings

In 1987 Forbes magazine listed Michael Jackson as the ninth highest paid entertainer, with two year estimated earnings of $34 million. In 1988 they listed him as the No.1 entertainer with earnings of $97 million. In the same year, during his 'Bad Tour', his European promoters revealed that Michael had negotiated a deal worth £20 million of which he receives 90% of all the proceeds from all the concert projects. After paying his entourage of one hundred and forty he was left with profits of around £400,000 per show.

## Recording Contract

In 1988 electronics giant Sony Software bought out Michael's record label CBS. In March 1991 Michael resigned his contract with the label which had been the biggest deal in musical history. The Japanese-owned multi-national corporation signed Michael to a 15 year, six album record and film contract which could be worth a potential $1 billion. Michael received an $18 million cash advance for the forthcoming album plus a $5 million bonus for his first and each of his subsequent five albums with the label.

Jackson was now the highest-paid entertainer in the music industry, receiving a royalty rate of 25% on each album sold.

## Record Label

Michael is also Chief Executive Officer of his own record label, Michael Jackson Music for which he receives $1 dollar per annum. The label now has four artists signed to it including the female trio Brownstone, male quartet Men Of Vision, and the young male trio 3T, which comprises his own nephews Taj, Taryll, and TJ.

## Film Company

In March 1993 Michael Jackson formed an independent film production company, Michael Jackson Productions which he claimed would produce uplifting movies, with a share of the profits going to his Heal The World foundation. Its first major project was a film about a killer whale entitled 'Free Willy'.

## Management

In 1997 Michael fired his long-time personal managers and put his career in the hands of Saudi Arabian Prince Alawaleed, who met Jackson in 1994 at Euro Disney.

Jackson and the Prince formed Kingdom Entertainment last year to develop films, TV shows, concerts, theme parks, hotels and restaurants.

# Michael the Family Man

We all know the public face of Michael Jackson but we know little of him behind closed doors. We know about his records and videos but what about his relationships? Let us start with his childhood, as the second youngest boy in the Jackson family.

## Childhood

Michael's childhood was one of perpetual work. Since his father Joe Jackson had realised that he himself would never make it as a recording star he lived his aspirations through his children. As well as the work Michael's predominant memories of his childhood are ones of fear. *"My father was real strict with us"*, Michael recalled, *"If you messed up you got hit, sometimes with a belt, sometimes with a switch."*

In his historic 1993 interview with Oprah Winfrey Michael revealed that he had been beaten as a child, although he had denied it when he was trying to patch things up with his father after 'Moonwalk'. *"I love my father,"* he said *"but I don't know him. To me my mother's just wonderful, she's perfection. I just wish I could understand my father. There were times when he would come to see me and I would get sick both as a child and as an adult."*

## Love Life

Oprah also asked Michael about his love life though he refused to talk about sex.

*"I'm a gentleman,"* he coyly answered. *"That is something that is private. Call me old fashioned. I'm embarrassed."* He counts many beautiful and famous women as his friends, like one of his early musical mentors Diana Ross, and actresses such as: Elizabeth Taylor, Jane Fonda, Sophia Loren and Liza Minnelli.

Over the years Michael has been seen out on the town with many other famous and beautiful women from the daughter of actor Ryan O'Neal, Tatum, to actress Brooke Shields, to singer Madonna. But none of them have ever been seriously linked with Michael romantically for any length of time. He did however admit on the Oprah interview that he was dating Brooke Shields, and that they met at their homes rather than go out because they might be spotted. *"Yes I've been in love,"* he shyly confessed, *"with Brooke and with someone else."* Though he revealed no more in that interview we discovered whom that someone else was just over a year later.

# Wife Number One

In February of 1994 Michael attended a concert by The Temptations at the Sheraton Desert Inn in Las Vegas. His date for the evening was Elvis Presley's daughter, Lisa Marie. In May, Star magazine reported that Lisa Marie had turned to Michael after the break up of her marriage to Danny Keough. In that same month Michael and Lisa Marie were married in a secret ceremony in the Dominican Republic. None of Michael's family was present and the wedding did not become public knowledge until GMTV broke the story in the UK in July.

It was not made official until August when Lisa Marie released a statement through Michael Jackson Productions. In it she stated that she was very much in love with Michael and wanted to dedicate her life to being his wife. Pleading for privacy Michael's 26 year old bride said that the news had been kept secret until now in the hopes of avoiding a media circus and so they could enjoy each other's company.

In August the two appeared on the covers of the National Enquirer, Jet and Hello magazine but it was not until October that Michael gave his first interview to Ebony magazine explaining the history of their relationship.

According to the article the two were just children when they first met in Las Vegas. He was 16 and she was 6 and the Jackson Five were performing at the MGM Grand Hotel in 1974. Her father Elvis would take her along to see the show and afterwards they would go backstage and meet the Jackson family. But it was not until the early 1990's when the duo met up again. They would talk on the phone and went out to a number of events together but kept their close friendship a secret. When the child abuse allegations broke in 1993 Lisa Marie was very supportive of Michael and they grew closer.

When news of their marriage became public the press were very sceptical, some even suggesting that it was a business move to unite the two great musical houses of Graceland and Neverland. Some even went so far as to suggest that it was a lavender wedding - a marriage of convenience for two public figures to cover the fact that one or more of them were gay.

In June 1995 the two appeared on ABC Television's Prime Time Live which was syndicated around the world. They talked of their hopes for children, their plans to move away from America and answered the cynics. Lisa Marie defended allegations that it was a marriage of convenience. *"Why would I marry somebody I didn't love? I admire him, I respect him, and I love him. He's in the studio, I'm in the kitchen. We run around the same house and we're normal people. And we don't sleep in separate bedrooms."*

However, despite their claims of undying love their marriage only lasted nineteen months. In January 1996 Lisa Marie filed for divorce citing irreconcilable differences. This only served to add strength to those doubters who had dismissed the marriage as a publicity stunt to detract attention away from the child abuse allegations.

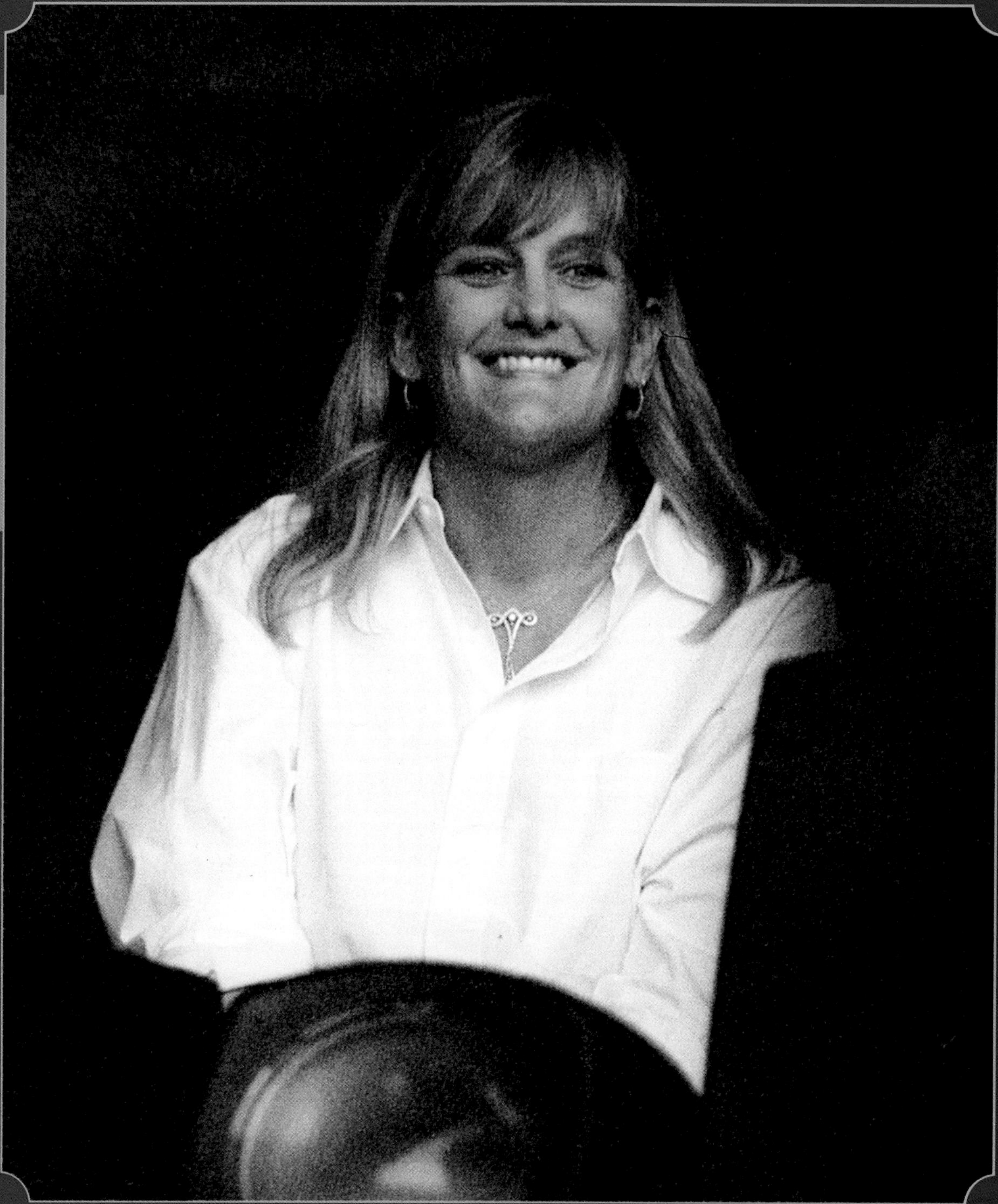

## Wife Number Two

By November of the same year Michael had married again - this time not to anyone remotely famous or glamorous but instead to 37 year old nurse, Debbie Rowe. They exchanged vows in a secret ceremony whilst Jackson was on the Australian leg of his HIStory tour. Michael issued a written statement at the time saying only: *"Please respect our privacy and let us enjoy this wonderful and exciting time."* The wedding took place only ten days after Michael announced that Rowe, a longtime friend, was pregnant and was due to give birth in early 1997. The two met whilst he was getting treated at the Arnold Klien Clinic, in Los Angeles where she worked. The two were reported to have been friends for fifteen years, but the couple became close when Debbie stood by Michael as he faced the allegations of child abuse.

## Prince Michael Junior.

Debbie gave Michael a son, his first child in February 1997. The boy was named Prince Michael Junior after Michael's grandfather and great-grandfather. Exclusive pictures of the child along with an interview with Michael and his second wife appeared in the April edition of OK magazine. *"Debbie and I love each other for all the things you will never see on stage or in pictures,"* said Michael in the interview. *"I fell for the beautiful, unpretentious giving person that she is, and she fell for me, just for being me".*

He denied a tabloid report that the couple used artificial insemination and that Rowe was paid $528,000 to carry the baby. Another tabloid, reported in December that Jackson would pay Rowe a $1.24 million fee when the child was born and $2.3 million for custody if their marriage breaks down. The condition of the big pay-off was that she never sees the child again, said yet another newspaper, quoting an insider source. But this was certainly not the impression that we got from the OK interview. *"I have married and had a baby with a man I will always love,"* said Debbie looking every bit the proud mother, *"and I am on top of the world."*

# Michael the Peter Pan

### Peter Pan

## "All children, except one, grow up."

This is the opening sentence of JM Barrie's timeless classic 'Peter Pan' - Michael's favourite book. It tells the story of the three children of Mr. and Mrs. Darling, Wendy, John and Michael, the dog Nana and the motherless Peter Pan - the boy who never grew up. In the story Peter Pan whisks the three children off to his home of Never Neverland where they have adventures with the Red Indians and Captain Hook and his Pirates. Whilst they stay in Never Neverland they will remain children but as appealing as this idea is, eventually they decide that they must return home and grow up.

The similarities between the fictional story of Peter Pan and the real life story of Michael Jackson are pretty compelling. It is often argued that because Michael grew up in the spotlight and had no real childhood of his own he is still living out his adolescent fantasies. *"All over the walls of my room are pictures of Peter Pan. I've read everything that Barrie wrote. I totally identify with Peter Pan, the lost boy from Never Neverland."*

Michael of course has named his ranch Neverland Valley Ranch and there was much talk in the mid 1980's of Michael playing the part in a movie of the story but eventually the starring role in the movie 'Hook' went to Robin Williams. *"When I'm upset about a recording session, I'll dash off on my bike and ride to the schoolyard, just to be around them."* said Michael in an early interview. *"When I come back to the studio, I'm ready to move mountains. Kids do that to me. It's like magic."*

## No Childhood

After receiving a Grammy Legend Award in 1993 he made this statement as part of his acceptance speech. *"My childhood was completely taken away from me. There was no Christmas there was no birthdays ...It was not a normal childhood. Those were exchanged for hard work, struggle, pain, and eventually material and professional success. But as an awful price I cannot recreate that part of my life.*

*"And that's why I love children and learn so much from being around them. I realise that many of the world's problems today, from inner city crime to large scale wars and terrorism, and our overcrowded prisons are a result of the fact that children have had their childhoods stolen from them. The magic, the wonder, the mystery and the innocence of a child's heart are the seeds of creativity that will heal the world. I really believe that. What we need to learn from children isn't childish. Being with them connects them to the deeper wisdom of life, which is ever present and only asks to be lived. They know the way to solutions that lie waiting to be recognised within our own hearts. Today I would like to thank all the children of the world including the sick and deprived. I am so sensitive to your pain."*

## Children's Movies

He is also a lover of children's films. One of his favourite films is ET.

*"The first time I saw ET I melted through the whole thing. The second time I cried like crazy."* In 1982 Michael went into the studio to narrate and sing on the Quincy Jones/ Steven Spielberg storybook record project, 'ET, The Extra Terrestrial'.

*"That's what I loved about doing ET,"* said Michael, *"I was actually there with them, like behind the tree or something, watching everything that happened. The next day I missed him a lot. I wanted to go back to that spot I was at yesterday in the forest. I wanted to be there."* He's also a big fan of cartoons. *"I'm a collector of cartoons. All the Disney stuff, Bugs Bunny, the old MGM ones. It's real escapism, it's like everything's alright. It's like the world is happening now in a far away city. Everything's fine."*

## Children's Charities

His love of children is well known. He has made many compassionate visits to sick children in hospitals over the years as well as making large charitable donations to children's charities. In 1989 he gave the proceeds from one of his LA shows to Childhelp USA, the largest non-profit child abuse prevention organisation in America. In recognition of Michael's contribution, Childhelp established the Michael Jackson International Institute For Research On Child Abuse. In the same year Say Yes To A Youngster honoured Michael for his role in encouraging school children to study mathematics and science by presenting him with the National Urban Coalition Artist/Humanitarian Of The Year Award.

In April 1993 Michael accepted a Caring For Kids Award, an award that acknowledges a celebrity who has devoted time to work with young people to enhance their lives. One hundred thousand children between the ages of 8 and 18 gave Michael their vote of confidence. During his world 'Bad Tour' he visited sick children in two wards at the Bambin Gesu Children Hospital in Rome signing autographs and handed out candy albums and tapes to the children.

Whilst in London he visited children at the Great Ormond Street hospital and presented a cheque to the Prince's Trust for £150,000 and a cheque to Great Ormond for £100,000. The proceeds for his concert in Leeds went to British charity Give For Life, the organisation whose goal was to raise £1 million towards immunising children. In December of 1988 reports appeared in the press that Michael had been making compassionate visits to the bedside of David Rothenburg, a 12 year old who was hospitalised after his father set him alight in an act of revenge against his estranged wife.

In February 1989 Michael Jackson visited the children of Cleveland Elementary School in Stockton, California, the scene of random shooting by a deranged man just a few weeks earlier.

At the end of 1989 Ryan White, a young haemophiliac who contracted the AIDS virus in 1984 from tainted blood products used to treat his condition, spent a vacation at Michael's Neverland Ranch. Michael gave his young guest a red Mustang car during the visit. When Ryan died in April 1990 Michael attended the funeral.

In August 1990 Michael Jackson invited one hundred and thirty children from the YMCA's summer program in Los Angeles to his ranch. He was made an honorary member of the 28th Street YMCA in Los Angeles.

In September 1990 the LA Council of Boy Scouts of America honoured Michael Jackson with the first ever Michael Jackson Good Scout Humanitarian Award.

He invited eighty-two abused and neglected children from Childhelp USA to Neverland Ranch. The two bus loads of children were treated to games, a barbecue and a private screening of 'The Little Mermaid' and 'Back To The Future Part II' in Michael's private cinema.

In February 1992 he announced plans for a new world tour to raise funds for his newly formed Heal The World foundation which contributes to Paediatric AIDS in memory of Ryan White, Camp Ronald McDonald, Make A Wish Foundation, Juvenile Diabetes and the Minority AIDS Foundation. In September 1992 during his 'Dangerous World Tour' he opened a playground for orphans in Romania. In November of 1992 Michael witnessed the loading of forty-three tons of medical supplies, blankets, winter clothing and shoes onto a DC-8 cargo jet bound for the children of Sarajevo in Bosnia-Herzegovina, a war zone in the former Yugoslavia. The Heal The World Foundation teamed up with the AmeriCares to fly the $2.1 million worth of aid to the Croatian capital, Zagreb, and then to Sarajevo for the distribution under the supervision of the UN High Command for Refugees.

In March 1995 he turned up unannounced at the funeral of Craig Fleming who died aged just 21 months old when his 24 year old mother threw him from the bridge in Los Angeles Harbour. In 1995 he also paid for the liver transplant of Bela Farkas a 5 year old Hungarian boy whom he met during a visit to Budapest in August 1994.

## Child Friends

Due to Michael's belief that the mind-state of children is so closely related to adult's creative state he surrounds himself with children and counts many as his friends.

Macaulay Culkin, star of the 'Home Alone' movies, was one of Michael's more famous child friends. Culkin starred in Michael's video for the song 'Black or White'.

Michael went on holiday to Bermuda with Macaulay Culkin and his parents. Culkin also spent his 11th birthday at the Neverland Ranch.

## Child Abuse Accusations

It was the close and intimate relationship that he had with many children that made him vulnerable to the accusations that he faced in 1993. In August the Los Angeles Police Department officially opened a criminal investigation on Jackson based on allegations of child abuse made by a 13 year old boy, Jordy Chandler. On December 22nd 1993 he went on TV and made this statement. *"Throughout my life, I have only tried to help thousands upon thousands of children to live happy lives. It brings tears to my eyes when I see any child who suffers. I am not guilty of these allegations. But if I am guilty of anything, it is of giving all that I have to give to help children all over the world. It is of loving children of all ages and races, it is of gaining sheer joy from seeing children with their innocent and smiling faces. It is of enjoying through them the childhood that I missed myself. If I am guilty of anything it is of believing what God said about children: 'Suffer little children to come unto me and forbid them not, for such is the Kingdom of Heaven.' In no way do I think that I am God, but I try to be God-like in my heart."*

In a television interview in 1995 with his new wife Lisa Marie Presley she went some way to explaining his relationship with children.

*"I've seen this,"* she said. *"I've seen it a lot. I have seen him with children in the last year. They don't let him go to the bathroom without running in. They won't let him out of their sight. They even jump into bed with him."*

January 1994 both sides in the child molestation allegation case reached an out of court settlement for an undisclosed sum.

## Christ-Like

Michael was involved in controversy again in 1996 when he performed 'Earth Song' at the British music awards ceremony The Brits. Michael was dressed all in white, singing whilst suspended above the stage in a high rise crane lift with a chorus of children singing below him on the stage, when Jarvis Cocker, the lead singer of the group Pulp, ran onto the stage flicking V-signs at Jackson. Cocker was swiftly tackled by security guards who injured three children in the process. Cocker explained his behaviour as a protest against Jackson's performance. He said at the time *"Michael Jackson sees himself as some Christ-like figure with the power of healing. The music industry allows him to indulge his fantasies because of his wealth and power."*

In June 1994 Country and Western music star Garth Brookes who works for Feed The Children said *"You can beat me up for this but who's raised more money for children than Michael Jackson has?"*

# What They Say

"He wasn't ever really interested in money. I'd give him his share of the night's earnings and the next day he'd buy ice cream or candy for all the kids in the neighbourhood."

*Father - Joe Jackson*

"He is very curious and wants to draw from people who have survived. People who have lasted the course. He is not really of this planet. If he is eccentric it is because he is larger than life.
"What is a genius? What is a living legend? What is a megastar? Michael Jackson - that's all. And just when you think you know him, he gives you more...There is no one that can come near him. No one can dance like that, write the lyrics or cause the kind of excitement that he does."

*Elizabeth Taylor on the booklet for 'HIStory'*

"He spends a lot of time, too much time by himself. I try to get him out. I rented a boat and took my children and Michael out on a cruise. Michael has a lot of people around him, but he's very afraid. I don't know why. I think it came from his early days."

*Diana Ross*

"Sure he's a little afraid of people. When you have people that from the time you're a little kid, want a part of you, they want your clothes, they want your hair - you're going to get a little nervous around people."

*Vince Paterson - choreographer*

"He wasn't at all sure that he could make it on his own. And me too. I had my doubts."

*Quincy Jones before Off The Wall*

# *About Michael*

"He can sing in front of 90,000 people but in front of three it's very difficult for him. We've sat in my studio when he was going to sing me a new song and I had to close my eyes and turn my back.

"What people forget about him is that for the first time, probably in the history of music, a Black artist is embraced on a global level by everyone from eight to eighty years old. People all over the world especially young people have a Black man as an idol."

*Quincy Jones - producer of Michael's first three solo albums*

"I didn't get destroyed by the press and fan mania and neither will Michael. He's very talented. He knows how to make records that people like. But he's a very straightforward kid. He has a great deal of faith. He's got a great deal of innocence and he protects that especially. Michael looks at cartoons all day and keeps away from drugs. That's how he maintains his innocence."

**Paul McCartney**

"His intelligence is instinctual and emotional, like a child's. If any artist loses that childlike innocence, you lose a lot of creative juice. So Michael creates around himself a world that protects that creativity."

*Jane Fonda*

"Just as Elvis Presley and The Beatles helped galvanise stagnating industries in their eras, so can Jackson help unify an audience large and diverse enough to count as a genuine mass consensus."

*Mikal Gilmore - Los Angeles Examiner 1983*

"I've recorded a whole lot of these pop musicians and Michael's the straightest of the goddamn lot. OK, Michael's got a few quirks but everybody in California does. O.K. so he's got his nose changed a bit. That's just normal in LA. I've looked in every room of that mansion of his for that oxygen tent that he's supposed to sleep in and it ain't in his bedroom. It ain't anywhere."

*Bruce Swedien - engineer on every Michael Jackson album*

"Michael as well as myself, have been severely underestimated and misunderstood as human beings. I can't wait for the day when the snakes who tried to take him out get to eat their own lunch and crawl back into the holes from which they came. We know who they are and their bluff is about to be called."

*Lisa Marie Presley in 1995 before their divorce*

"People always ask me is he weird? We'll he's different. But I know what it's like to be weird growing up in the music industry."

*Slash Guns & Roses guitarist (played on 'Dangerous' and 'HIStory' albums)*

"This LP shows Michael's strength of character. He has risen out and above all the rubbish that was printed and said about him. He has matured as a man and as a vocalist too. The emotion with which he sings is unreal, a true singer of songs, and I know of no other performer in the world who could match what Michael has achieved with this recording."

*Bruce Swedien on 'HIStory'*

# Michael Jackson
# Chronological Biography!

**Aug 29th 1958**   Michael Joseph Jackson is born in Gary, Indiana.

**1964**   Michael Jackson becomes the lead singer of the Jackson Five aged only 6.

**May 1968**   Jackson Five win Apollo Theatre Talent Contest.

**Winter 1968**   Jackson Five are signed to Motown.

**Dec 1969**   Jackson Five's first album is released.

**Mar 1970**   'ABC' is released.

**June 1970**   'The Love You Save' hits the No.1 spot.

**June 1972**   Michael Jackson releases his first solo album 'Got To Be There'.

**Oct 1972**   Releases 'Ben' his first US No.1 solo single.

**Late 72-early 73**   Jackson Five tour the world.

**1976**   Jackson Five become The Jacksons and record their first album 'The Jacksons' for Epic Records.

**1978**   Michael Jackson stars as the Scarecrow in the movie musical 'The Wiz'.

**Sep 1978**   'Blame It On The Boogie' hits the US Top Ten.

**1979**   'Off The Wall' is released on Epic, becoming one of the most successful albums of the year and later earning him his first Grammy Award. It had five hit singles in Britain and went onto sell 11 million copies.

**1980**   The Jacksons get together to record another album, 'Triumph'.

**Dec 1982**   'Thriller' is released. It goes on to be the most successful album of all time selling 50 million copies.

**Jan 1983**   The single 'Billie Jean' reaches No.1 in the UK.

**Dec 1983**   The Michael Jackson Suite is opened at the Royal Plaza Hotel in Florida's Disney World.

# Discography

**Jan 1984**    Michael Jackson suffers second degree burns whilst filming a Pepsi television advertisement.

**Feb 1984**    Michael Jackson gets a record breaking eight Grammy Awards.

**Nov 1984**    Michael Jackson unveils his star on the Hollywood Boulevard Walk of Fame.

**1984**    Michael Jackson gets back with the Jacksons to record the 'Victory' album.

**July - Sep 84**    'The Victory Tour'.

**Aug 1985**    Michael Jackson buys the ATV publishing catalogue, which includes most of Lennon and McCartney's music.

**Sep 1986**    'Captain EO', Michael Jackson's 17 minute space fantasy premieres at the Epcot Centre in Disney World Florida.

**Sep 1987**    'Bad' is released. The first album to yield five No.1's in the US. Selling four million copies in the UK and twenty-five million world-wide it is the second biggest selling album of all time.

**Sep 1987**    'World Bad Tour' opens in Japan playing one hundred and twenty-three dates in fifteen countries on four continents.

**Apr 1988**    'Moonwalk' Michael Jackson's autobiography is released. Within two weeks it is top of the UK Best Sellers List.

**May 1988**    Michael Jackson moves from his parents home to the Sycamore Ranch in Santa Ynez Valley. It is soon renamed the Neverland Valley Ranch.

**Dec 1988**    'Moonwalker' Michael Jackson's first major movie is released in cinemas.

**Feb 1989**    The single 'Leave Me Alone' makes UK No.1.

**Sep 1991**    MTV renames the Video Vanguard Award, the Michael Jackson Video Vanguard Award in honour of his great achievement in this field.

**Mar 1991**    Michael Jackson signs a new contract with the Sony Corporation signing him to a 15 year six album record and film contract known as the billion dollar deal.

**Nov 1991** 'Dangerous' is released. It goes on to sell 20 million copies.

**Dec 1992** 'Heal the World' hits UK No.1.

**Jan 1993** Michael Jackson performs at the Superbowl halftime show.

**Feb 1993** Michael Jackson gives a rare interview to Oprah Winfrey in America.

**Mar 1993** Forms an independent film company, Michael Jackson Productions.

**July 1993** 'Free Willy' with Michael Jackson's 'Will You Be There'; as it's theme song opens in cinemas in the US.

**Aug 17th 1993** The LAPD officially open a criminal investigation on Michael based on allegations of child abuse made by 13 year old boy Jordy Chandler.

**Dec 22nd 1993** Michael Jackson goes on TV to make a public statement regarding the allegations.

**Jan 1994** Both sides in the child molestation allegations reach an out of court settlement for an undisclosed sum.

**May 1994** Michael Jackson marries Lisa Marie Presley in the Dominican Republic.

**June 1995** Michael Jackson and Lisa Marie give a joint TV interview to ABC that is syndicated around the world.

**June 1995** 'HIStory' is released. It goes onto sell 14 million copies.

**Jan 1996** Michael Jackson and Lisa Marie divorce.

**Nov 1996** Michael Jackson marries 37 year old nurse Debbie Rowe in Australia.

**Feb 1997** Michael Jackson and Debbie have a son, Prince Michael Junior.

**April 97** 'Blood On the Dancefloor' enters the UK Singles chart at No.1.

**May 1997** Michael Jackson's film 'Ghost' is premiered in London and at the Cannes Film Festival. 'Blood On the Dancefloor'-'HIStory In The Mix' is released and goes straight to No.1.